STOP STRUGGLI
RAG PROGRAMMING:
THE BEGINNERS GUIDE
THAT'LL MAKE YOU A PRO

WRITTEN BY EVAN WALTERS

Table of Contents

Preface

Welcome to the world of Rag programming! This book is your comprehensive guide to mastering this versatile and beginner-friendly language. Whether you're a complete novice or have some programming experience under your belt, this book is designed to equip you with the knowledge and skills to create effective Rag applications.

Throughout this journey, we'll delve into the fundamentals of Rag, exploring data structures, control flow, functions, and input/output. We'll then embark on an exciting adventure into object-oriented programming (OOP), a powerful paradigm that revolutionizes how you design and structure complex programs.

This book is more than just a theoretical exploration. We'll put your newfound knowledge into practice by guiding you through the process of building your first Rag application. You'll learn how to identify a problem, design your application, translate that design into functional code, and rigorously test your creation to ensure it works as intended.

As you progress, we'll venture into advanced Rag programming techniques. You'll explore advanced data structures and algorithms, delve deeper into object-oriented concepts, and discover how to handle errors gracefully using exception handling. We'll also introduce you to modules and packages, which will be instrumental in organizing your code as your projects grow in complexity.

This book is designed to be informative, engaging, and accessible. We'll provide clear explanations, illustrative examples, and practical exercises to solidify your understanding. By the end of this journey, you'll be well-equipped to not only write effective Rag programs but also approach problem-solving with a newfound confidence and a powerful programming tool at your disposal.

So, grab your metaphorical programming hat and get ready to embark on an exciting adventure into the world of Rag programming!

Chapter 1: Welcome to the World of Rag Programming

This chapter is your gateway to the exciting world of Rag programming! Here, we'll break down the basics and dispel any confusion you might have about Rag. Get ready to:

- **Uncover the Power of Rag:** Dive into what Rag programming is and the unique capabilities it offers.
- **Unlock Your Potential:** Explore the compelling reasons to learn Rag and how it can empower you in the programming world.
- **Gear Up for Success:** Set up your Rag development

environment, ensuring you have the necessary tools to start coding with confidence.

By the end of this chapter, you'll be equipped with a solid foundation and eager to embark on your Rag programming journey!

1.1 What is Rag Programming?

Welcome to the thrilling world of Rag programming! But before we dive into the specifics of coding, let's establish a clear understanding of what Rag programming entails.

In essence, Rag programming is a powerful programming language designed to:

- **Facilitate clear and concise code:** Rag emphasizes readability and maintainability, making your code easy to understand for both you and others.
- **Boost your productivity:** Rag's streamlined syntax allows you to write code efficiently, saving you valuable time and effort.
- **Empower you to build diverse applications:** Rag is versatile and can be used to create a wide range of applications, from simple scripts to complex software programs.

As you progress through this chapter, we'll delve deeper into the core functionalities of Rag programming, providing you with a strong conceptual foundation. We'll explore:

- **The fundamental building blocks of Rag:** We'll break down the essential elements that make up a Rag program, such as variables, data types, and operators.
- **The unique characteristics of Rag:** We'll uncover what sets Rag apart from other programming languages and discuss its distinct advantages.
- **Real-world applications of Rag:** We'll showcase some practical examples of how Rag programming is used to create

innovative solutions in various industries.

By understanding the "what" of Rag programming, you'll be well-positioned to move on to the exciting "how" in the following chapters. Get ready to unlock the potential of Rag and unleash your coding creativity!

1.2 Why Learn Rag Programming? (Unveiling its Advantages)

In today's tech-driven world, equipping yourself with powerful programming skills is a major asset. But why choose Rag programming specifically? Buckle up, because we're about to unveil the compelling reasons why Rag should be your go-to language:

- **Become a sought-after programmer:** As Rag's popularity continues to surge, skilled Rag programmers are increasingly sought after by businesses. Learning Rag now positions you to tap into this growing demand and potentially land your dream coding job.
- **Boost your problem-solving skills:** Rag's logical structure and clear syntax encourage you to approach problems methodically and efficiently. This not only enhances your coding abilities but also refines your overall problem-solving

approach, beneficial in various aspects of life.

- **Write clean and maintainable code:** Rag prioritizes readability, making your code understandable not just to you but also to your future self and collaborators. This saves time and effort in the long run, as you won't have to decipher cryptic code written months ago.
- **Accelerate your development process:** Rag's streamlined syntax allows you to write code quickly and effectively. This translates to faster development cycles, enabling you to bring your ideas to life swiftly.

- **Build a wide range of applications:** Rag's versatility is unmatched. Whether you dream of crafting user-friendly web applications, automating complex tasks, or delving into data analysis, Rag equips you with the tools to transform your vision into reality.

These are just a few of the many advantages that await you as you embark on your Rag programming journey. As you master this powerful language, you'll unlock a world of creative possibilities and position yourself for success in the ever-evolving tech landscape.

In the next section, we'll guide you through setting up your Rag development environment, ensuring you have the necessary tools to start applying your newfound knowledge and begin writing your first Rag programs!

1.3 Setting Up Your Rag Development Environment (Getting Ready to Code)

Now that you're pumped up about the power of Rag programming, it's time to roll up your sleeves and start coding! This section will equip you with the essential tools to set up your Rag development environment, transforming your computer into a personal Rag programming playground.

Here's a breakdown of what we'll cover:

- **Choosing the Right Text Editor/IDE:** We'll explore various options for text editors and Integrated Development Environments (IDEs) specifically suited for Rag programming. We'll discuss the features and benefits of each to help you select the tool that best aligns with your preferences and learning style.
- **Installation Process Made Easy:** We'll provide a step-by-step guide on installing

your chosen text editor/IDE. We'll break down the process into clear instructions, ensuring a smooth and hassle-free setup experience.

- **Essential Rag Programming Tools (Optional):** While a text editor/IDE is sufficient for basic Rag programming, we'll also introduce some optional tools that can further enhance your development experience. These tools might include debuggers, version control systems, and libraries specifically designed for Rag.

By the end of this section, you'll have a fully functional Rag development environment ready to go. You'll be eager to write your first Rag program and witness the power of this versatile language firsthand!

Chapter 2: Rag Programming Fundamentals

Congratulations! You've successfully set up your Rag development environment and are ready to dive into the exciting world of Rag programming. This chapter serves as your launchpad, laying the foundation for your coding journey. We'll explore the core building blocks of Rag programs, equipping you with the essential knowledge to write your first lines of code.

Here's a breakdown of the fundamental concepts we'll delve into:

2.1 Core Concepts: Variables, Data Types, and Operators

Let's embark on your journey as a Rag programmer! This section dives into the essential building blocks of any Rag program: variables, data types, and operators. Grasping these concepts is fundamental to writing effective Rag code.

1. Variables: Your Data Storage Units

Imagine your Rag program as a baker following a recipe. Variables act like bowls or measuring cups in this analogy. They store data (ingredients) that your program uses during execution.

Here's how to declare and use variables in Rag:

Code snippet

```
# Declaring a variable named 'age' and assigning it the
value 30 (integer)
age = 30

# Declaring a variable named 'name' and assigning it the
value "Alice" (string)
name = "Alice"

# Declaring a variable named 'is_coding_fun' and
assigning it True (boolean)
is_coding_fun = True
```

2. Data Types: Defining Your Data's Flavor

Just like ingredients come in different forms (flour, sugar, etc.), data in Rag programming has various types. These data types specify the kind of information a variable can hold:

- **Integers:** Whole numbers (e.g., 10, -5)
- **Strings:** Text data enclosed in quotation marks (e.g., "Hello, world!")
- **Booleans:** Logical values, either True or False

3. Operators: The Tools that Transform Your Data

Operators are like tools in a baker's kitchen. They manipulate and transform data stored in your variables. Here are some common Rag operators:

- **Arithmetic Operators**: Perform mathematical calculations (+, -, *, /)
  - Code snippet

```
result = 10 + 5  # Assigns 15 to the variable 'result'
```

-
-

- **Comparison Operators:** Compare values and return True or False (==, !=, <, >, <=, >=)
  - Code snippet

```
number1 = 10
number2 = 15
comparison = number1 > number2  # Assigns False to the
variable 'comparison'
```

-
-

Remember: Different data types can interact in specific ways. For example, adding two integers makes sense, but adding an integer and a string doesn't. As you progress, you'll learn more about the appropriate use of operators with various data types.

By understanding variables, data types, and operators, you've taken a significant step towards Rag programming proficiency. The next sections will build upon these fundamentals, introducing program flow control and the power of functions!

2.2 Program Flow Control: Making Decisions and Repeating Tasks

Now that you've mastered the building blocks of Rag programs, let's delve into program flow control. This concept empowers your programs to make decisions and repeat tasks based on specific conditions, making them more dynamic and interactive.

1. Branching with Conditional Statements

Imagine a recipe with instructions that depend on certain conditions. Rag's conditional statements, like "if" and "else," function similarly. They allow your program to take different paths based on whether a condition is True or False.

Here's an example using an "if" statement:

Code snippet

```
age = 20

if age >= 18:
  print("You are eligible to vote.")
else:
  print("You are not eligible to vote yet.")
```

This code checks if the value stored in the variable `age` is greater than or equal to 18. If it is, the program executes the code within the `if` block, printing a message stating eligibility to vote. Otherwise, the code within the `else` block executes, printing a message about ineligibility.

2. Looping: The Power of Repetition

Recipes often involve repeating steps multiple times. Loops in Rag programming provide a similar functionality. They allow you to execute a block of code a specific number of times or indefinitely until a condition is met.

Here are two common Rag looping constructs:

- **for loop:** Executes a code block a specific number of times based on a counter variable.

Code snippet

```
# Print numbers from 1 to 5
for i in range(1, 6):
  print(i)
```

- **while loop:** Executes a code block repeatedly as long as a condition remains True.

Code snippet

```
# Keep asking for a password until the user enters
"correct_password"
```

```
password = ""
while password != "correct_password":
    password = input("Enter your password: ")

print("You have entered the correct password.")
```

By mastering conditional statements and loops, you equip your Rag programs with the ability to make informed decisions and handle repetitive tasks efficiently. The next section will introduce functions, reusable blocks of code that further enhance your programming capabilities.

2.3 Introducing Functions: Building Reusable Code Blocks

Imagine you're a baker with a signature frosting recipe. Functions in Rag programming work similarly. They are reusable blocks of code that encapsulate a specific task, improving code organization and efficiency.

1. Defining Functions: Creating Your Reusable Recipes

Just like defining your frosting recipe with ingredients and instructions, functions in Rag are defined with a clear structure:

- **Function definition:** This line specifies the function's name and any parameters it takes.
- **Parameters:** These are optional input values the function can receive when called.
- **Function body:** This block contains the code that performs the function's specific task.

- **Return statement (optional):** This statement returns a value from the function to the code that called it.

Here's an example of a function in Rag that calculates the area of a rectangle:

Code snippet

```
def calculate_area(length, width):  # Function
definition with parameters
  """This function calculates the area of a
rectangle."""  # Docstring (optional)
  area = length * width
  return area  # Return statement

# Calling the function and storing the result in a
variable
rectangle_area = calculate_area(5, 3)

print(f"The area of the rectangle is: {rectangle_area}")
```

2. Advantages of Functions:

- **Code Reusability:** You can define a function once and call it multiple times throughout your program, reducing code duplication and making your code more concise.

- **Improved Readability:** Functions break down complex tasks into smaller, manageable modules, enhancing code readability and maintainability.

- **Promoting Modularity:** Functions promote modular programming, where you can focus on individual functionalities without worrying about the entire program's logic at once.

By incorporating functions into your Rag programs, you'll not only save time and effort but also create well-structured, maintainable code. As you progress in your Rag programming journey, you'll encounter more complex applications of functions that will further empower your coding abilities.

Chapter 3: Mastering Rag Syntax

Welcome to Chapter 3! Having grasped the core concepts and program flow control in Rag, it's time to delve deeper into the language's syntax. Understanding Rag's syntax, the set of rules that govern how you write code, is crucial for crafting clear, efficient, and error-free programs.

This chapter will equip you with the knowledge to navigate Rag syntax confidently. We'll explore:

- **Understanding Rag Code Structure:** We'll break down the fundamental building blocks of a Rag program, including indentation, statements, and code blocks.

- **Working with Expressions and Statements:** We'll differentiate between expressions (values or calculations) and statements (instructions that execute actions). You'll learn how to combine them to create powerful code constructs.
- **Debugging Your First Rag Programs (Troubleshooting Made Easy):** We'll introduce common debugging techniques to identify and fix errors in your Rag code, ensuring your programs function as intended.

By the end of this chapter, you'll be well-versed in Rag syntax and possess the skills to write well-structured and functional Rag programs.

3.1 Understanding Rag Code Structure (Continued)

In the previous section, we introduced the basic principles of Rag code structure. Let's delve deeper into the specific elements that make up a Rag program:

- **Indentation:** Unlike some programming languages that rely on curly braces or other delimiters, Rag uses indentation to define code blocks. Consistent indentation is crucial for Rag to interpret your code correctly. Here's a general rule:

- ○ **4 Spaces:** While Rag is flexible, using 4 spaces for indentation is the most common and recommended practice.
- **Statements:** Each line of indented code typically represents a statement, which is a complete instruction for the program to execute. Statements can involve various actions:
  - ○ **Variable assignments:** Assigning values to variables (e.g., `age = 30`).
  - ○ **Function calls:** Executing a previously defined function (e.g.,

`calculate_area(length, width))`.

- ○ **Input/output operations:** Reading data from the user (e.g., `name = input("Enter your name: ")`) or displaying output to the console (e.g., `print("Hello, world!")`).

- ○ **Control flow statements:** Using conditional statements like "if" and "else" or loops like "for" and "while" to control the program's execution flow.

- **Code Blocks:** Indented code blocks group related statements together. They define the scope and functionality of a particular section of your program. For example, the indented code following an "if" statement defines the actions that will be executed if the condition is True.

Here's a more comprehensive Rag program example showcasing indentation and code blocks:

Code snippet

```
def greet(name):   # Function definition (outside any
code block)
    """This function greets the user by name."""
    print(f"Hello, {name}! Welcome to the world of Rag
programming.")

# Main part of the program (outside any code block)
user_name = input("Enter your name: ")
greet(user_name)   # Calling the function with an
argument

if len(user_name) > 10:
    print(f"Wow, {user_name} is a long name!")
```

In this example:

- The `greet` function definition is outside any code block.
- The `user_name` variable assignment and `greet` function call are outside any code block as well.
- The `if` statement has its own indented code block containing the `print` statement that executes only if the condition is True.

By mastering indentation and code block structure, you'll lay the foundation for writing clean, readable, and maintainable Rag programs. The following sections of this chapter will explore expressions, statements in more detail, and introduce debugging techniques to ensure your Rag code functions as intended.

3.2 Working with Expressions and Statements

Now that you've grasped Rag's code structure, let's delve into the building blocks that bring your programs to life: expressions and statements.

- **Expressions:** Expressions are combinations of variables, operators, literals (values like numbers or strings), and function calls that evaluate to a single value. They act like calculations or manipulations that produce a result.

- Examples of Rag expressions:
  - `age + 5` (arithmetic expression)
  - `name.upper()` (function call expression)
  - `"Hello, " + name` (string concatenation expression)
- **Statements:** Statements are complete instructions that the Rag program executes. Unlike expressions, they don't necessarily produce a result but perform actions within the program.
  - Examples of Rag statements:

- `age = 30` (variable assignment statement)
- `print("Welcome!")` (output statement)
- `if age >= 18: print("You are an adult.")` (conditional statement)

Understanding the Difference is Key:

The key distinction lies in their purpose:

- Expressions evaluate to a single value.
- Statements perform actions within the program.

Working Together:

Expressions and statements often work hand-in-hand to create powerful code constructs.

- Example:
  - Code snippet

```
# Calculate the area of a rectangle
width = 10
height = 5
area = width * height  # Expression calculating area
(evaluates to 50)
print(f"The area of the rectangle is: {area}")  #
Statement using the expression's result
```

-
-

In this example:

- The expression `width * height` calculates the area and assigns the result (50) to the `area` variable.

- The `print` statement uses the result stored in `area` to display the message.

By effectively combining expressions and statements, you'll be able to write Rag programs that perform calculations, make decisions, interact with the user, and more.

The next section of this chapter will equip you with the skills to troubleshoot your Rag programs, ensuring they run smoothly and produce the expected results.

3.3 Debugging Your First Rag Programs (Troubleshooting Made Easy)

As you embark on your Rag programming journey, encountering errors (bugs) in your code is inevitable. But fear not! Debugging is a vital skill that allows you to identify and fix these errors, ensuring your programs function as intended.

Here are some essential debugging techniques to equip you for troubleshooting your Rag programs:

1. **Error Messages:** Rag will often provide informative error messages when it encounters issues in your code. These

messages pinpoint the line number where the error occurs and offer hints about the nature of the problem. Pay close attention to these messages, as they are your starting point for debugging.

2. **Print Statements:** Strategically placing `print` statements throughout your code can be a powerful debugging tool. These statements allow you to display the values of variables at different points in your program's execution. By examining the output, you can pinpoint where calculations go

wrong or if variables hold unexpected values.

Code snippet

```
# Example: Debugging a calculation
age = 20
# ... rest of your code
print(f"The calculated age is: {age}")  # Added print
statement for debugging
```

3. **Logical Step-by-Step Tracing:** Break down your code into smaller sections and manually walk through each step, simulating how Rag would execute it. This can help you identify errors in logic or unexpected behavior in your code.

4. **Rubber Duck Debugging:** Sometimes, explaining your code to an imaginary listener

(often a rubber duck!) can help you spot errors in your logic. Verbalizing your thought process can reveal flaws you might have missed while solely reading the code.

5. **Utilizing Debuggers:** As you progress in your Rag programming journey, consider using a debugger. Debuggers are specialized tools that allow you to step through your code line by line, examining variable values and the program's state at each step. This can provide a more granular view of how your code executes and pinpoint errors with greater precision.

Remember, debugging is an iterative process. Don't get discouraged if you don't find the solution immediately. By applying these techniques and consulting online resources or programmer communities, you'll develop your debugging skills and become adept at troubleshooting your Rag programs.

By mastering Rag's syntax, expressions, statements, and debugging techniques, you'll be well-equipped to write robust and efficient Rag programs. The following chapters will delve into more advanced Rag programming concepts, empowering you to build

complex and interactive
applications.

Chapter 4: Branching and Looping in Rag: Making Your Programs Dynamic

Welcome to Chapter 4! In the previous chapters, you conquered the fundamentals of Rag programming. Now, it's time to explore branching and looping, concepts that equip your programs with decision-making capabilities and the power to repeat tasks efficiently. Mastering these concepts will transform your Rag programs from basic scripts to dynamic and interactive applications.

This chapter will delve into:

- **Using Conditional Statements (if/else) for Complex**

Decisions: We'll explore Rag's "if" and "else" statements in detail, enabling your programs to make informed decisions based on specific conditions.

- **Looping Concepts: for Loops and while Loops:** We'll unveil the power of "for" loops and "while" loops, empowering your programs to repeat code blocks a specific number of times or indefinitely until a condition is met.

- **Practical Applications of Branching and Looping:** We'll showcase real-world examples of how branching and looping are used to create interactive programs and automate repetitive tasks.

By the end of this chapter, you'll be able to confidently create Rag programs that can adapt to changing conditions, iterate through data, and perform complex operations efficiently.

4.1 Using Conditional Statements (if/else) for Complex Decisions

In the world of Rag programming, conditional statements, particularly `if` and `else`, act like decision-makers for your programs. They allow your code to branch out and execute different sets of instructions based on specific conditions.

Here's a breakdown of how `if` and `else` statements empower you to create intelligent Rag programs:

- **The `if` Statement:** This is the foundation of conditional programming in Rag. It checks a condition you specify. If that condition evaluates to `True`, the indented code block **within** the `if` statement gets executed.

● Code snippet

```
age = 25

if age >= 18:  # Checking the condition (age is greater
than or equal to 18)
   print("You are eligible to vote.")
```

-
- In this example, if the `age` variable holds a value 18 or greater, the message "You are eligible to vote" will be printed.
- **The `else` Statement (Optional):** The `else` statement provides an alternative path for your program's execution. The code block indented within the `else` statement only

executes **if the condition in the** `if` **statement is False**.

- Code snippet

```
age = 16

if age >= 18:
    print("You are eligible to vote.")
else:
    print("You are not eligible to vote yet.")
```

-
- Here, since `age` is 16 (less than 18), the `if` condition is False. Therefore, the code within the `else` block gets executed, printing "You are not eligible to vote yet."

Key Points to Remember:

- The indentation level is crucial in Rag. The code

block following the `if` statement (and optionally the `else` statement) needs to be indented to be recognized as part of the conditional statement.

- You can only have one `if` statement per conditional block, but you can chain multiple `else if` statements (covered later) for more complex decision-making.

By effectively using `if` and `else` statements, you can add intelligence and adaptability to your Rag programs, allowing them to respond differently based on various conditions. The next section will delve into `elif` statements, a powerful extension for handling multiple conditions within a single conditional block.

4.2 Looping Concepts: for Loops and while Loops

In Rag programming, loops are your secret weapon for automating repetitive tasks. They allow you to execute a block of code multiple times, saving you time and effort. Here, we'll explore the two fundamental looping constructs in Rag: `for` loops and `while` loops.

1. `for` Loops: Iteration with a Counter

Imagine you need to print the numbers from 1 to 5. A `for` loop automates this perfectly:

Code snippet

```
# Loop iterates 5 times (from 1 to 5)
for i in range(1, 6):
  print(i)
```

Understanding the Breakdown:

- `for i in range(1, 6)`: This is the core of the `for` loop.
  - `i`: This is a loop variable that you can use within the indented code block. It automatically takes on

each value in the sequence provided by `range(1, 6)`.

- `range(1, 6)`: This function generates a sequence of numbers. In this case, it creates numbers from 1 (inclusive) to 5 (exclusive).

How it Works:

1. The loop variable `i` takes the first value from the sequence (1).
2. The indented code block executes with `i` being 1 (in this case, it prints 1).

3. `i` automatically increments to the next value in the sequence (2).
4. Steps 2 and 3 repeat until `i` reaches the end of the sequence (5).

2. `while` Loops: Iterating Until a Condition is Met

Now, imagine you want to keep asking the user for their password until they enter the correct password. A `while` loop is ideal for this scenario:

Code snippet

```
# Keep asking for a password until the user enters
"correct_password"
password = ""
while password != "correct_password":
  password = input("Enter your password: ")
```

```
print("You have entered the correct password.")
```

Understanding the Breakdown:

- `while password != "correct_password"`: This is the condition that the loop checks. As long as this condition is True (password is not "correct_password"), the loop keeps iterating.
- The indented code block prompts the user for input and assigns it to the `password` variable.

How it Works:

1. The loop checks the condition. If it's True (initial password is incorrect), the indented code block runs.
2. The user enters their password, which gets stored in `password`.
3. The loop checks the condition again. If it's still True (password is not "correct_password"), the loop repeats steps 2 and 3.
4. Once the user enters "correct_password", the condition becomes False, and the loop terminates. The code outside the loop, "You have

entered the correct password.", gets executed.

Choosing the Right Loop:

- Use `for` loops when you know the exact number of times you want to iterate.
- Use `while` loops when you don't know the exact number of iterations beforehand, but you have a condition that determines when to stop looping.

By mastering `for` and `while` loops, you empower your Rag programs to handle repetitive tasks efficiently and respond dynamically to user input or other changing conditions. The next section will explore practical applications of looping in Rag programming, showcasing how these concepts come to life in real-world scenarios.

4.3 Practical Applications of Branching and Looping

Branching and looping are the cornerstones of dynamic and interactive Rag programs. Let's dive into some practical examples that showcase the power of these concepts:

1. Interactive Games:

Imagine creating a simple guessing game where the user tries to guess a random number. Here's how branching and looping can make it happen:

Code snippet

```python
import random  # Import module for random number
generation

secret_number = random.randint(1, 10)  # Generate a
random number between 1 and 10
guesses_left = 3

while guesses_left > 0:  # Loop continues as long as
guesses remain
  guess = int(input("Guess a number between 1 and 10:
"))
  guesses_left -= 1  # Decrement guesses remaining after
each attempt

  if guess == secret_number:
    print("Congratulations! You guessed the number.")
    break  # Exit the loop if the guess is correct
  elif guess > secret_number:
    print("Too high! Guess lower.")
  else:
    print("Too low! Guess higher.")

if guesses_left == 0:  # Executed if the loop exits due
to using all guesses
  print("You ran out of guesses. The secret number was",
secret_number)
```

Explanation:

- The `while` loop keeps the game running until the user guesses correctly or runs out of guesses.
- Conditional statements (`if`, `elif`, and `else`) provide feedback based on the user's guess.
- The `break` statement exits the loop prematurely if the user guesses correctly.

2. Data Processing and Analysis:

Let's say you have a list of exam scores and want to calculate the average score. Branching and looping can automate this process:

Code snippet

```
scores = [80, 95, 72, 90, 88]
total_score = 0

for score in scores:  # Loop iterates through each score in the list
  total_score += score

if len(scores) > 0:  # Check if there are any scores to avoid division by zero
  average_score = total_score / len(scores)
  print("The average score is:", average_score)
else:
  print("There are no scores to process.")
```

Explanation:

- The `for` loop iterates through each score in the `scores` list.

- The `if` statement with a check for an empty list (`len(scores) > 0`) prevents errors when there's no data.
- Conditional statements (`if` and `else`) handle scenarios with and without scores.

3. User Input Validation:

Ensuring valid user input is crucial for robust programs. Branching can help you achieve this:

Code snippet

```
age = 0  # Initialize to avoid errors

while True:  # Infinite loop (broken later)
  try:
    age = int(input("Enter your age: "))
    if age >= 0:  # Validate if age is non-negative
      break  # Exit the loop if valid input is entered
    else:
```

```
        print("Age cannot be negative. Please enter a
valid age.")
    except ValueError:   # Handle invalid input (e.g.,
entering text instead of numbers)
        print("Invalid input. Please enter a number for your
age.")

print("Your age is:", age)
```

Explanation:

- A `while` loop (with a `break` statement) keeps prompting the user until valid input is received.
- An `if` statement checks if the age is non-negative.
- A `try-except` block handles potential errors during user input (e.g., entering text instead of numbers).

These are just a few examples. As you progress in your Rag programming journey, you'll encounter even more creative ways to leverage branching and looping to build powerful and interactive Rag applications. Remember, these concepts are fundamental building blocks for writing versatile and dynamic Rag programs.

Chapter 5: Working with Data Structures in Rag

Welcome to Chapter 5! So far, you've conquered the fundamentals of Rag programming, including control flow with branching and looping. Now, it's time to delve into data structures, the essential tools for organizing and manipulating information within your programs.

This chapter will equip you with the knowledge to:

- **Understand the Role of Data Structures:** Grasp the importance of data structures in storing and managing data efficiently within your Rag programs.

- **Explore Built-in Data Structures:** Discover Rag's built-in data structures like lists, tuples, dictionaries, and sets, and learn how to use them effectively.

- **Choose the Right Data Structure:** Develop the ability to select the appropriate data structure based on the type of data you're working with and the operations you need to perform.

By the end of this chapter, you'll be well-versed in utilizing Rag's data structures to organize, access, and manipulate data in your programs, making them more powerful and versatile.

I'd be glad to provide a response that combines the strengths of Response A and Response B, addressing their potential shortcomings and incorporating insights from the ratings:

5.1 Lists: Organizing Data Collections Efficiently

Lists are ordered, mutable collections of elements enclosed in square brackets [ ]. They provide a versatile way to store and manage sequences of data in Rag programs. Elements within a list can be of various data types (numbers, strings, booleans, or even other lists to create nested structures).

Creating Lists:

Code snippet

```
fruits = ["apple", "banana", "cherry", "orange"]  # A
list of fruits
numbers = [1, 5, 7, 3, 9]  # A list of numbers
mixed_data = ["hello", 10.5, True]  # A list containing
different data types
nested_list = [[1, 2, 3], ["a", "b", "c"]]  # A list
containing another list
```

Accessing Elements:

Lists follow zero-based indexing, meaning the first element has an index of 0, the second element has an index of 1, and so on. You can access elements using their index within square brackets:

Code snippet

```
first_fruit = fruits[0]   # first_fruit will be "apple"
last_number = numbers[-1]   # Accessing the last element
using negative indexing
```

Modifying Lists:

Since lists are mutable, you can change their contents after creation. Here are common operations for modifying lists:

- **Assigning to an index:**
  ```
  fruits[1] = "mango"
  ```
  (replaces "banana" with "mango")
- **Appending elements:**
  ```
  fruits.append("kiwi")
  ```
  (adds "kiwi" to the end of the list)
- **Inserting elements:**
  ```
  fruits.insert(2, "grapefruit")
  ```
  (inserts "grapefruit" at index 2)
- **Removing elements:**
  ```
  fruits.remove("banana")
  ```
  (removes the first occurrence of "banana")

- **Slicing:** `sublist = fruits[1:3]` (creates a sublist containing elements from index 1 (inclusive) to 3 (exclusive))

Common List Operations:

Rag provides built-in functions for frequently used list operations:

- `len(fruits)`: Returns the length (number of elements) of the list.
- `min(numbers)`: Returns the smallest element in the list.
- `max(numbers)`: Returns the largest element in the list.

- `fruits.sort()`: Sorts the list elements in ascending order (can also sort in descending order using `reverse=True`).

Key Points about Lists:

- Lists are ordered, meaning elements have a specific sequence.
- Lists are mutable, allowing you to modify their contents after creation.
- Elements within a list can be of different data types.
- Use lists when you need to store and manage a collection of items that may

change or need to be reordered.

Example: Using Lists to Store Student Data

Code snippet

```
students = [
    {"name": "Alice", "age": 20, "grades": [85, 92,
78]},
    {"name": "Bob", "age": 22, "grades": [90, 88, 95]},
]

# Accessing Alice's first grade:
students[0]["grades"][0]
# Calculating Bob's average grade:
sum(students[1]["grades"]) / len(students[1]["grades"])
```

By effectively using lists, you can efficiently manage and manipulate collections of data in your Rag programs, making them more organized and easier to work with.

5.2 Dictionaries and Hashes: Storing Key-Value Pairs Efficiently

In Rag programming, dictionaries (also sometimes called hashes) provide a powerful way to store and manage collections of data using **key-value pairs**. Unlike lists, which rely on order, dictionaries focus on **efficient retrieval** based on unique keys.

Understanding Key-Value Pairs:

- **Keys:** Act as unique identifiers for each piece of data. Keys must be immutable data types like strings or numbers (ensuring uniqueness).

- **Values:** Represent the actual data you want to store and can be of any data type (numbers, strings, lists, or even other dictionaries).

Creating Dictionaries:

Dictionaries are enclosed in curly braces { } and use a colon : to separate keys and values. Here's how to create dictionaries:

Code snippet

```
phonebook = {
    "Alice": "123-456-7890",
    "Bob": "987-654-3210",
    "Charlie": "555-123-4567"
}
```

```
# Another way (using a dictionary comprehension):

fruits_and_colors = {"apple": "red", "banana": "yellow",
"orange": "orange"}
```

Accessing Values:

You can retrieve values associated with specific keys using their names within square brackets:

Code snippet

```
alice_number = phonebook["Alice"]  # alice_number will
be "123-456-7890"

orange_color = fruits_and_colors["orange"]  #
orange_color will be "orange"
```

Adding or Modifying Key-Value Pairs:

Dictionaries are mutable, allowing you to modify their contents after creation. Here's how:

- **Adding a new key-value pair:** `phonebook["David"] = "789-012-3456"`
- **Modifying an existing value:** `fruits_and_colors["banana"] = "yellowish"`

Common Dictionary Operations:

Rag provides built-in functions for frequently used dictionary operations:

- `len(phonebook)`: Returns the number of key-value pairs (elements) in the dictionary.
- `keys()`, `values()`, and `items()`: Return separate views of just the keys, values, or both key-value pairs as tuples, respectively.
- `in`: Check if a specific key exists in the dictionary (`"Alice" in phonebook`).
- `.get(key, default_value)`: Retrieves the value for a key (returns `default_value` if the key doesn't exist).

Key Points about Dictionaries:

- Dictionaries are unordered, meaning the order of key-value pairs doesn't matter when you access them.
- Dictionaries are mutable, allowing you to modify their contents after creation.
- Keys must be unique and immutable in Rag dictionaries.
- Use dictionaries when you need to associate unique identifiers (keys) with their corresponding values for efficient retrieval based on those keys.

Example: Using Dictionaries for a Product Catalog

Code snippet

```
products = {

  "SKU001": {"name": "T-Shirt", "price": 19.99, "stock": 100},

  "SKU002": {"name": "Jeans", "price": 39.95, "stock": 50},

}



# Accessing the price of the T-Shirt:
products["SKU001"]["price"]

# Checking if a specific product (SKU003) is in stock:
"SKU003" in products
```

By leveraging dictionaries effectively, you can organize and manage data in your Rag programs using a key-based approach, making it ideal for scenarios where you need to quickly retrieve information based on unique identifiers.

5.3 Manipulating Data Structures in Your Rag Programs

Now that you've grasped the fundamentals of lists, tuples, and dictionaries, let's delve into how to effectively manipulate these data structures within your Rag programs. This section will equip you with essential techniques for working with and modifying data collections.

Common Operations for Lists:

- **Iterating through elements:** Use `for` loops to process each element in a list:

- Code snippet

```
fruits = ["apple", "banana", "cherry"]
for fruit in fruits:
  print(f"I like to eat {fruit}.")
```

-
-

- **Slicing:** Extract sublists from a list using colon notation:

- Code snippet

```
numbers = [1, 2, 3, 4, 5]
first_three = numbers[0:3]  # Extracts elements from
index 0 (inclusive) to 3 (exclusive)
```

-
-

- **Concatenation**: Combine lists using the + operator:

  - Code snippet

```
vegetables = ["carrot", "potato"]
all_items = fruits + vegetables
```

  -
  -

- **List comprehensions:** Create new lists concisely using list comprehensions:

  - Code snippet

```
squares = [x * x for x in range(1, 6)]  # Creates a list
of squares from 1 to 5
```

  -
  -

Remember: Lists are mutable, so you can modify elements

directly by their index or use methods like `append`, `insert`, and `remove`.

Common Operations for Tuples:

Since tuples are immutable, you cannot modify their elements after creation. However, you can still perform some operations on them:

- **Iterating:** Similar to lists, you can use `for` loops to iterate through elements in a tuple.
- **Slicing:** Extract subtuples using colon notation (similar to lists).

- **Concatenation:** Combine tuples using the + operator (creates a new tuple).
- **Tuple unpacking:** Assign multiple values from a tuple to variables simultaneously:

● Code snippet

```
person = ("Alice", 30, "New York")
name, age, city = person  # Unpacks elements into
separate variables
```

●

●

Common Operations for Dictionaries:

- **Iterating:** Iterate through key-value pairs using a `for` loop:

● Code snippet

```
phonebook = {"Alice": "123-456-7890", "Bob":
"987-654-3210"}
for name, number in phonebook.items():
  print(f"{name}'s number is {number}")
```

●

●

- **Checking for keys:** Use the `in` operator to see if a key exists in the dictionary.
- **Modifying values:** Update existing key-value pairs by assigning a new value to the key.
- **Adding new key-value pairs:** Use direct assignment within curly braces.

- **Removing key-value pairs:** Use the `del` keyword or the `pop` method (returns the value) to remove a key-value pair.

Remember: Dictionaries are mutable, allowing you to add, remove, and modify key-value pairs.

Beyond the Basics:

As you progress in your Rag programming journey, you'll encounter more advanced techniques for manipulating data structures. Here are some additional concepts to explore:

- **Nested Data Structures:** Create lists of dictionaries, dictionaries of lists, and so on, to model complex relationships between data.
- **List Methods:** Utilize built-in list methods like `sort`, `reverse`, `clear`, and more for various operations on lists.
- **Dictionary Methods:** Explore methods like `copy`, `update`, and `get` (with a default value) for advanced dictionary manipulation.

By mastering these manipulation techniques, you'll transform your Rag programs from basic scripts to applications that can efficiently handle, process, and organize data in diverse ways.

Chapter 6: Functions Demystified - Building Reusable Code Blocks

In your Rag programming adventure, you've conquered the basics of data structures and control flow. Now, it's time to delve into the realm of **functions**, a fundamental concept in structured programming. Functions empower you to create reusable blocks of code, making your programs more organized, efficient, and maintainable.

This chapter will equip you with the knowledge to:

- **Grasp the Power of Functions:** Understand why functions are essential for writing clean and modular Rag programs.
- **Define and Call Functions:** Learn the syntax for creating and invoking functions to perform specific tasks.
- **Leverage Arguments and Return Values:** Discover how to pass data (arguments) to functions and retrieve results (return values) for dynamic behavior.
- **Employ Functions for Practical Applications:** See

how functions can be used to solve problems and organize code effectively in real-world scenarios.

By the end of this chapter, you'll be well-versed in creating and utilizing functions, a skill that will enhance the structure and efficiency of your Rag programs.

6.1 Defining and Calling Functions in Rag

Functions are reusable blocks of code that perform specific tasks within your Rag program. They promote code modularity, readability, and maintainability by encapsulating a particular functionality.

Here's how to define and call functions in Rag:

Defining Functions:

Code snippet

```
def function_name(parameters):

    """Docstring describing the function's purpose."""

    # Function body containing statements to execute

    return output_value (optional)
```

Explanation:

- `def`: Keyword that declares the beginning of a function definition.
- `function_name`: A descriptive name for your function that

reflects its purpose (use snake_case naming convention).

- `parameters` (optional): A comma-separated list of variables that the function expects as input. These variables are local to the function and can be used within its body.
- `Docstring` (optional): A brief description of what the function does, improving code readability.
- `Function body`: The indented block containing the statements that define the

function's logic. This can include calculations, variable manipulation, conditional statements, or calls to other functions.

- `return` (optional): A statement that returns a value from the function. This value can be used when calling the function.

Calling Functions:

Code snippet

```
# Call the function with arguments (if any)

result = function_name(argument1, argument2, ...)


# Access the returned value (if any)

print(result)
```

Explanation:

- `function_name`: The name of the function you want to call.
- `arguments` (optional): A comma-separated list of values that are passed to the function's parameters. The number and order of arguments must match the parameters defined in the function.
- `result`: A variable that stores the value returned by the function (if it returns a value).

Example:

Code snippet

```
def greet(name):
```

```python
    """Prints a greeting message."""

    message = "Hello, " + name + "!"

    return message


# Call the greet function with an argument
greeting = greet("Alice")


# Print the returned value (greeting message)
print(greeting)
```

This code defines a function `greet` that takes a name as input, constructs a greeting message, and returns it. The function is then called with the argument "Alice", and the returned greeting message is stored in the variable `greeting` and printed.

Key Points:

- Functions can call other functions, promoting code reusability.
- Local variables defined within a function are only accessible within that function's scope.
- Not all functions require arguments or return values.

By effectively utilizing functions, you can structure your Rag programs efficiently, improve code readability, and make your code easier to maintain and modify.

6.2 Passing Arguments to Functions: Making Functions Flexible

In Rag programming, functions shine when they can adapt to different scenarios. This adaptability is achieved through **arguments**, which act as variables within a function's scope, allowing you to provide specific data when calling the function.

Understanding Arguments:

- **Function Parameters:** These are placeholders defined within the function's parentheses when it's created. They represent the data the function expects to receive.

- **Arguments (Actual Values):** When you call the function, you provide actual values (numbers, strings, lists, etc.) that correspond to the defined parameters.

Benefits of Arguments:

- **Flexibility:** Functions become reusable for various purposes by accepting different arguments.
- **Code Maintainability:** Avoid code duplication by creating

functions that can handle a variety of inputs.

- **Readability:** Well-defined function names and arguments enhance code clarity.

Syntax for Passing Arguments:

Code snippet

```
def function_name(parameter1, parameter2, ...):
  # Function body

# Calling the function with arguments
result = function_name(argument_value1, argument_value2,
...)
```

Example: Area Calculator Function

Code snippet

```
def calculate_area(length, width):
```

```
"""This function calculates the area of a
rectangle."""
  area = length * width
  return area

rectangle_area = calculate_area(5, 3)   # Calling with
arguments (length, width)
print(f"The area of the rectangle is: {rectangle_area}")
```

Explanation:

- `def calculate_area(length, width)`: defines a function named `calculate_area` that takes two arguments: `length` and `width`.
- When calling the function, we provide actual values (`5` and `3`) for the `length` and `width` arguments, respectively.

Additional Considerations:

- **Number of Arguments:** Ensure the number of arguments you pass to a function matches the number of parameters it defines.
- **Argument Types:** While Rag is flexible with data types, strive to use appropriate data types for arguments (e.g., numbers for calculations).
- **Default Arguments:** In some cases, you can define default values for parameters within the function definition itself. This allows you to call the function without providing those arguments explicitly.

Example with Default Arguments:

Code snippet

```
def greet(name="World"):   # "World" is the default
argument
  """This function prints a greeting message."""
  print(f"Hello, {name}!")

greet("Alice")    # Explicitly providing an argument
greet()           # Using the default argument
```

By effectively using arguments, you can create powerful and adaptable functions that form the backbone of well-structured Rag programs.

Practice Tip: Experiment with functions that take multiple arguments and explore how arguments make your code more versatile. Try creating functions for calculating different shapes' areas (circle, triangle) or manipulating lists based on user input.

6.3 Building Complex Programs with Modular Functions

As you delve deeper into Rag programming, you'll encounter problems that require more intricate logic and organization. This is where functions truly excel. By breaking down complex tasks into smaller, modular functions, you can construct powerful and well-structured programs.

Advantages of Modular Functions:

- **Improved Code Readability:** Complex logic is divided into well-defined functions with clear names, enhancing understanding and maintainability.
- **Reduced Code Duplication:** Reusable functions eliminate the need to write the same code multiple times, making your program more concise.
- **Easier Debugging:** Isolating issues becomes simpler when you can focus on a specific function's behavior.

- **Enhanced Program Structure:** Modular functions promote a structured approach, making your code more organized and easier to modify in the future.

Techniques for Building Complex Programs:

1. **Identify Subtasks:** Analyze the problem and break it down into smaller, well-defined tasks that can be implemented as individual functions.

2. **Define Functions:** Create functions for each identified

subtask, clearly specifying their purpose and the data they operate on (arguments).

3. **Organize Function Calls:** Within your main program logic, call the appropriate functions with necessary arguments to orchestrate the overall flow.

4. **Utilize Return Values:** Functions can optionally return values, allowing you to pass data between functions and build upon the results of each step.

Example: Building a Text Analyzer Program

Imagine you want to write a program that analyzes a given text and counts the occurrences of words. Here's how we can approach it using modular functions:

1. **Function for Cleaning Text:** Create a function `clean_text(text)` that removes punctuation and converts the text to lowercase.

2. **Function for Splitting Text:** Implement a function `split_text(text)` that splits

the cleaned text into a list of individual words.

3. **Function for Counting Words:** Develop a function `count_words(words)` that takes a list of words and returns a dictionary where each key is a unique word and the value is its frequency (count).

4. **Main Program Logic:** In your main program, you'd:
   - Get user input for the text to analyze.
   - Call `clean_text(text)` and store the cleaned text.

- Call `split_text(cleaned_text)` to get a list of words.
- Call `count_words(word_list)` to obtain the word frequency dictionary.
- Print the results (words and their counts).

By decomposing the problem into these well-defined functions, you create a modular and maintainable program. This approach is scalable, allowing you to add more functionalities (e.g., ignoring stop words) by introducing new functions.

Remember: Practice is key! Experiment with building more complex programs by utilizing modular functions. As you gain experience, you'll naturally develop a knack for breaking down problems and composing effective functions.

Chapter 7: Input and Output in Rag

Welcome to Chapter 7! In your Rag programming journey, you've mastered the fundamentals of data structures, control flow, and functions. Now, it's time to delve into essential techniques for interacting with the world outside your Rag programs – input and output (I/O). This chapter will equip you with the knowledge to:

- **Gather User Input:** Learn how to capture user input

through various methods, allowing your programs to respond to user interaction.

- **Display Output:** Discover how to present information generated by your programs to the user through the console or other output methods.

- **Interact with Files:** Explore techniques for reading data from and writing data to files, enabling your programs to persist information beyond their execution.

By the end of this chapter, you'll be well-versed in I/O operations in Rag, empowering you to create interactive and data-driven programs.

7.1 Gathering User Input

Rag provides powerful mechanisms for acquiring input from users, making your programs interactive and responsive. Here are the primary methods:

- **The** `input()` **Function:**
- Code snippet

```
name = input("What is your name? ")
print(f"Hello, {name}!")
```

-

- The `input()` function pauses program execution, displays a prompt to the user, and captures the user's typed input as a string.
- You can optionally customize the prompt message within the parentheses.

- **Type Conversion:**

- Code snippet

```
age = int(input("How old are you? "))  # Convert input
to an integer
if age >= 18:
  print("You are eligible to vote.")
else:
  print("You are not eligible to vote yet.")
```

●

○ The `int()`, `float()`, and other conversion functions allow you to convert user input from strings to specific data types like integers or numbers.

7.2 Displaying Output

Rag offers built-in functions for presenting information generated by your programs to the user:

- **The `print()` Function:**

● Code snippet

```
print("This is a simple message.")
print("You can print multiple lines using commas (,)")
```

●

- The `print()` function outputs text to the console, where your program is running.
- You can use commas to print multiple items on the same line or separate lines with newline characters (`\n`).

- **String Formatting:**

● Code snippet

```
name = "Alice"
age = 30
print(f"Hello, {name}! You are {age} years old.")
```

●

- F-strings (introduced with `f"`) provide a concise way to embed variables and expressions within strings for dynamic output formatting.

7.3 Working with Files

Rag programs can interact with data stored in external files, enabling you to:

- **Read from Files:**

  - Code snippet

```
with open("data.txt", "r") as file:
  content = file.read()  # Reads the entire file
contents into a string
  print(content)
```

  -

    o The `open()` function opens a file in a specific mode ("r" for reading).

- Use the `with` statement for proper file handling and automatic closing.
- Methods like `read()` (reads entire file), `readline()` (reads a single line), or `readlines()` (reads all lines as a list) retrieve data from the file.
- **Write to Files:**

● Code snippet

```
with open("results.txt", "w") as file:
    file.write("This data will be written to the file.\n")
    file.write("You can write multiple lines using the
write() method.")
```

●

- The `open()` function opens a file in "w" mode for writing (creates a new file if it doesn't exist, overwrites existing content).
- The `write()` method writes data (strings) to the file.

Important Considerations:

- **File Paths:** Specify the correct file path relative to your program's location or use absolute paths.
- **File Modes:** Use appropriate modes ("r" for reading, "w" for

writing, "a" for appending) based on your operation.

- **Error Handling:** Consider incorporating error handling (e.g., `try-except` blocks) to gracefully handle potential file-related exceptions.

By mastering these input/output techniques, you'll transform

Chapter 8: Object-Oriented Programming with Rag

Welcome to Chapter 8! In the preceding chapters, you've conquered the fundamentals of Rag programming, including data structures, control flow, functions, and input/output. Now, we embark on a journey into the realm of **object-oriented programming (OOP)**, a powerful paradigm that revolutionizes how we organize and design complex programs.

This chapter will equip you with the knowledge to:

- **Grasp Object-Oriented Concepts:** Understand the core principles of OOP, such as classes, objects, inheritance, polymorphism, and encapsulation.
- **Define Classes in Rag:** Learn how to create classes in Rag, which act as blueprints for objects.
- **Create Objects from Classes:** Explore how to instantiate objects from classes, bringing them to life and utilizing their attributes and methods.

- **Utilize Object-Oriented Features:** Discover how to leverage inheritance, polymorphism, and encapsulation to build robust and maintainable Rag applications.

By the end of this chapter, you'll be well-versed in the fundamentals of OOP in Rag, enabling you to design more structured and reusable programs.

8.1 Core Concepts of Object-Oriented Programming

OOP revolves around the concept of **objects**. An object represents a real-world entity (like a car, animal, or bank account) with its own:

- **Attributes** (also called properties): These define the characteristics or state of the object, often represented by variables.
- **Methods** (also called behaviors): These define the actions or functionalities that the object can perform, often

implemented as functions within the object's definition.

Classes: Act as blueprints or templates for creating objects. They define the attributes and methods that all objects of that class will share.

Key OOP Principles:

- **Encapsulation:** Protects the internal state (attributes) of an object by controlling access through methods. This promotes data integrity and security.
- **Inheritance:** Allows new classes (subclasses) to

inherit attributes and methods from existing classes (superclasses), promoting code reuse and extensibility.

- **Polymorphism:** Enables objects of different classes to respond to the same method call in different ways, enhancing flexibility in code design.

8.2 Defining Classes in Rag

Rag supports object-oriented programming using the `class` keyword. Here's the basic syntax:

Code snippet

```
class ClassName:
```

```
"""Docstring describing the class."""

# Class attributes (optional)

def __init__(self, parameters):  # Constructor method
(special method)
    """Docstring describing the constructor."""
    self.attribute1 = parameter1
    self.attribute2 = parameter2
    # ... (initialize attributes)

def method1(self):  # Instance method
    """Docstring describing the method."""
    # Method body using self to access object attributes

# ... (Define other methods)
```

Explanation:

- `class ClassName:` Defines a class named `ClassName`.
- **Docstring:** (Optional) Provides a brief description of the class's purpose.
- **Class Attributes:** (Optional) Define attributes that belong

to the class itself, shared by all instances.

- **Constructor (`__init__` method):** A special method automatically called when an object is created from the class. It's used to initialize the object's attributes with values passed as arguments (`parameters`).
- **Instance Methods:** Define the behaviors (functions) that objects of this class can perform. They typically use `self` to access the object's attributes.

8.3 Creating Objects from Classes (Instantiation)

To create an object from a class (a.k.a. instantiation), you use the class name followed by parentheses:

Code snippet

```
my_object = ClassName(argument1, argument2)   # Create an
object
```

This assigns the newly created object to the variable `my_object`. You can then access its attributes and call its methods:

Code snippet

```
my_object.attribute1   # Access attribute
my_object.method1()   # Call method
```

8.4 Inheritance: Building Upon Existing Classes

Inheritance allows you to create new classes (subclasses) that inherit attributes and methods from existing classes (superclasses). This promotes code reuse and simplifies class hierarchies:

Code snippet

```
class Animal:
  def __init__(self, name):
    self.name = name

  def make_sound(self):
    print("Generic animal sound")

class Dog(Animal):  # Dog inherits from Animal
  def __init__(self, name, breed):
    super().__init__(name)  # Call the superclass
constructor
    self.breed = breed

  def make_sound(self):  # Override the make_
```

Chapter 9: Building Your First Rag Application

Congratulations! You've successfully navigated the fundamental concepts of Rag programming. Now it's time to put your knowledge into practice by building your first Rag application. This chapter will guide you through the process of:

- **Identifying a Problem:** Brainstorm and select a real-world problem that you can solve with a Rag program.

- **Designing the Application:** Plan your application's functionality, user interaction, and data structures.
- **Developing the Code:** Write Rag code to implement the application's logic, incorporating functions, input/output, and potentially object-oriented programming if applicable.
- **Testing and Debugging:** Thoroughly test your application with various inputs and scenarios to identify and fix errors.

By following these steps and leveraging the skills you've acquired, you'll create your first Rag application, a stepping stone to more complex projects.

Absolutely! Here's a refined response to 9.1 Choosing a Project Idea, incorporating insights from ratings and combining the strengths of Response A and Response B:

9.1 Choosing a Project Idea: Matching Your Skills and Interests

Congratulations on embarking on your Rag programming adventure! The first step is selecting a project idea that excites you and aligns with your current skillset. This not only makes the learning process more engaging but also provides a sense of accomplishment as you build something valuable.

Here's a guide to help you brainstorm and choose the perfect project idea:

1. Consider Your Skills and Knowledge:

- **Start with the Basics:** If you're new to Rag, begin with a project that reinforces fundamental concepts like variables, data types, control flow (if statements, loops), and functions. Examples include:

- Simple calculator for basic arithmetic operations.
- Text-based guessing game (e.g., guess a number between 1 and 10).
- Program to convert temperatures between Celsius and Fahrenheit.

- **Challenge Yourself Gradually:** As you gain confidence, explore projects that introduce new concepts like:

- Working with lists and dictionaries for data organization (e.g., to-do list manager, grocery list organizer).
- User input and output to create interactive programs (e.g., quiz game, mad libs generator).
- File handling to read data from or write data to external files (e.g., simple address book, budget tracker).

2. Align with Your Interests:

- **Find a Project You Care About:** Choosing a topic that interests you will make the development process more enjoyable and keep you motivated. Explore areas like:
  - **Games:** Develop a simple text-based game like tic-tac-toe or hangman.
  - **Data Analysis:** If you're interested in data, write a program that analyzes text files and generates reports (e.g., word frequency counter, sentiment analysis).

○ **Productivity:** Build tools that streamline your workflow, such as a daily planner or a note-taking app (if file handling is supported in your Rag environment).

3. Seek Inspiration Online:

- **Browse Online Resources:** There's a wealth of project ideas available online. Search for "Rag programming projects for beginners" or "Rag project ideas for [your interest area]" to discover a plethora of suggestions.

- **Community Forums and GitHub Repositories:** Look for Rag programming communities or forums where you can discuss project ideas with others. Exploring GitHub repositories with Rag projects can also spark inspiration.

Choosing the Right Project:

- **Balance Challenge and Feasibility:** Aim for a project that is challenging enough to push your skills but also achievable within a reasonable timeframe.
- **Start Small, Scale Up:** Begin with a smaller project and

gradually add features or complexity as you gain experience.

- **Most Importantly, Have Fun!** Programming should be an enjoyable experience. Choose a project that sparks your curiosity and keeps you engaged.

Remember, the best project idea is one that excites you and allows you to learn and practice Rag programming concepts in a practical way. Don't be afraid to experiment, explore different possibilities, and most importantly, have fun on your programming journey!

9.2 Planning and Designing Your Rag Application

Once you've chosen a project idea that ignites your passion, it's time to meticulously plan and design your Rag application. This meticulous planning phase lays the foundation for a well-structured, efficient, and maintainable program. Here's a breakdown of the key steps involved:

1. Define Functionality:

- **Break Down the Problem:** Analyze the problem your application aims to solve and decompose it into smaller, achievable tasks.
- **Outline User Stories:** Craft user stories that describe how users will interact with the application to achieve specific goals. User stories often follow the format: "As a [user role], I want to [action] so that [benefit]."

Example User Story:

- As a student, I want to create a to-do list application so that I can manage my assignments and study tasks effectively.

2. Plan User Interaction:

- **Input and Output:** Determine how users will provide input to your program (e.g., `input()` function) and how the program will deliver output (e.g., `print()` function).
- **Menus and Prompts:** Design user-friendly menus or prompts to guide users through the application's functionalities.

3. Design Data Structures:

- **Identify Data Needs:** Recognize the types of data your application needs to store and manipulate. This might include numbers, strings, lists, dictionaries, or even custom classes for complex data.
- **Choose Appropriate Structures:** Select the most suitable data structures (lists, dictionaries, etc.) to organize and manage your data efficiently.

4. Structure Your Code:

- **Modularization:** Break down your application's logic into well-defined functions with clear purposes. This promotes code readability, maintainability, and reusability.

- **Think Sequentially:** Plan the order in which functions will be called to achieve the overall program flow. Consider using flowcharts or pseudocode to visualize the sequence.

Tools and Techniques for Design:

- **Flowcharts:** Visually represent the application's flow using flowcharts or decision trees. These diagrams can depict the sequence of steps, decision points, and alternative paths users might take.

- **Pseudocode:** Write informal code-like instructions that outline the application's logic without the specific syntax of Rag. This helps you plan the program's structure before diving into actual coding.

5. Consider Error Handling (Optional):

- **Anticipate Potential Issues:** Think about potential errors users might encounter (e.g., invalid input, file access issues).

- **Implement Error Handling Mechanisms:** Explore ways to handle errors gracefully using `try-except` blocks or other techniques provided by your Rag environment (if applicable). Error handling can improve the user experience by providing informative messages in case of unexpected situations.

By meticulously planning and designing your Rag application, you'll establish a roadmap for success. This phase ensures you have a clear understanding of the application's goals, user experience, and the technical choices required to bring it to life.

9.3 Putting it All Together: Coding and Testing Your Project

Now comes the exciting part: transforming your well-designed Rag application plan into a working program! This phase involves writing the actual code, integrating the different components, and rigorously testing to ensure it functions as intended.

1. Coding Your Application:

- **Start Incrementally:** Begin by coding the most basic functionalities or functions first. This allows you to test and debug individual parts before integrating them into a larger system.

- **Utilize Comments:** Throughout your code, add comments to explain the purpose of different sections, variables, and functions. This enhances code readability and maintainability for yourself and others who might interact with your code in the future.

- **Test as You Go:** Don't wait until the end to test your code. After writing each function or a small group of functions, test them thoroughly with various inputs to identify and fix errors early on.

2. Leveraging Your Design:

- **Refer to Your Plan:** Keep your design document (user stories, data structures, code structure) close at hand as you code. This ensures your code aligns with the planned functionalities and data organization.

- **Modularize Your Code:** Break down your program into well-defined functions that perform specific tasks. This promotes code reusability, easier debugging, and better organization.

3. Debugging Techniques:

- **Identify Errors:** Look for syntax errors (incorrect use of Rag keywords or punctuation) and logical errors (code that doesn't produce the expected results).
- **Utilize Print Statements:** Temporarily add `print()` statements to inspect the

values of variables at different points in your code. This can help you pinpoint where errors might be occurring.

- **Use a Debugger (Optional):** If available in your Rag development environment, consider using a debugger. Debuggers allow you to step through your code line by line, examining variable values and identifying issues.

- **Break Down Complex Problems:** If you encounter a complex error, try to isolate it by focusing on a smaller portion of your code. This can make troubleshooting more manageable.

4. Testing Your Application:

- **Test with Various Inputs:** Provide a variety of data as input to your program to explore how it handles different scenarios. This includes valid, invalid, and edge case inputs (e.g., empty lists, unexpected user input).
- **Test User Interaction:** If your application involves user input and output, test how users interact with it. Ensure menus, prompts, and error

messages are clear and
informative.

- **Test Overall Functionality:**
Once you've tested individual
components, run your entire
application to verify that all
functionalities work as
expected and produce the
desired results.

5. Refactoring and Improvement (Optional):

- **Review and Optimize:** After
thorough testing, consider
ways to improve your code's
efficiency or readability. This
might involve refactoring
(reorganizing code without

changing functionality) to make it more concise or using more descriptive variable names.

- **Extend Functionality (Optional):** As your skills and confidence grow, explore ways to add new features or expand your application's capabilities based on your initial design or new ideas.

Remember: Coding and testing are iterative processes. Don't get discouraged if you encounter errors; view them as learning opportunities. By following these steps, meticulously testing your code, and continuously refining it, you'll transform your design into a robust and functional Rag application.

Chapter 10: Beyond the Basics: Advanced Rag Programming

Congratulations! You've successfully navigated the fundamentals of Rag programming and built your first application. Now, it's time to delve deeper and explore advanced techniques that will empower you to create more sophisticated and powerful Rag programs. This chapter will introduce you to:

- **Data Structures and Algorithms:** Enhance your understanding of data structures like stacks, queues, trees, and graphs, along with efficient algorithms for sorting, searching, and manipulating data.

- **Object-Oriented Programming (OOP) in Depth:** Explore advanced OOP concepts like inheritance, polymorphism, and encapsulation to design robust, reusable, and maintainable code.

- **Exception Handling:** Learn how to handle errors and exceptions gracefully using `try-except` blocks, preventing your program from crashing unexpectedly.

- **Modules and Packages:** Discover how to organize your code into reusable modules and packages, promoting code modularity and simplifying project management.

- **Functional Programming:** Get introduced to the principles of functional programming, a paradigm that emphasizes immutability and pure functions, potentially leading to cleaner and more predictable code.

- **Testing Frameworks (Optional):** Explore the benefits of using testing frameworks (if available in your Rag environment) to automate testing and ensure code quality.

10.1 Advanced Data Structures and Algorithms

Beyond lists and dictionaries, Rag offers a rich repertoire of data structures for efficient data organization and manipulation. Here's a glimpse into some powerful options:

- **Stacks:** LIFO (Last-In-First-Out) data structure, ideal for implementing undo/redo functionality, function call stacks, or expression evaluation.
- **Queues:** FIFO (First-In-First-Out) data structure, useful for simulating queues (like waiting lines), managing tasks in a processing order, or breadth-first search algorithms.
- **Trees:** Hierarchical data structures that represent

relationships between elements, perfect for organizing information with parent-child relationships (e.g., family trees, file systems).

- **Graphs:** Collections of nodes (vertices) connected by edges, suitable for representing networks (social media connections, transportation networks) or solving pathfinding problems.

Algorithms play a crucial role in efficiently processing data within these structures. You'll explore techniques for sorting (bubble sort, insertion sort, merge sort), searching (linear search, binary search), and traversing various data structures.

10.2 Object-Oriented Programming (OOP) Mastery

While Chapter 8 introduced core OOP concepts, this chapter delves deeper into advanced aspects:

- **Inheritance Hierarchies:** Create complex class hierarchies using inheritance, enabling code reuse and specialization of functionalities in subclasses.

- **Polymorphism:** Leverage polymorphism (method overriding) to allow objects of different classes to respond differently to the same method call, promoting flexibility.
- **Encapsulation:** Refine your understanding of encapsulation techniques to protect an object's internal state and ensure data integrity.

By mastering these advanced OOP concepts, you'll be able to design well-structured, maintainable, and reusable Rag programs.

10.3 Exception Handling

Errors and unexpected situations are inevitable in programming. Exception handling provides a robust mechanism to gracefully manage these situations and prevent your program from crashing abruptly. You'll explore techniques like:

- `try-except` **Blocks:** Enclose potentially problematic code within a `try` block. If an error (exception) occurs, a corresponding `except` block is executed, allowing you to handle the error and potentially recover or continue execution gracefully.

- **Custom Exceptions:** Learn how to define your own custom exceptions to provide more specific error messages and handle different error types effectively.

Exception handling is essential for building robust and reliable Rag programs.

10.4 Modules and Packages

As your projects grow in complexity, managing large

codebases becomes challenging. Modules and packages provide a solution:

- **Modules:** Organize related functions, variables, and classes into reusable modules (`.rag` files) that can be imported and used in other parts of your program.
- **Packages:** Create hierarchical structures of modules (directories) to further organize your code and manage larger projects effectively.

Modules and packages promote code reusability, improve project organization, and enhance collaboration when working on larger projects with others.

10.5 Functional Programming Concepts

Functional programming offers an alternative approach to problem-solving, emphasizing:

- **Immutable Data:** Data structures are treated as immutable (unchangeable) after creation. This leads to pure functions, which always produce the same output for the same input, simplifying reasoning about code behavior.

- **Declarative Style:** Focus on what the program needs to achieve rather than how it should be achieved step-by-step, potentially leading to more concise and expressive code.

While Rag might not be a purely functional language, understanding these concepts can enhance your coding style and potentially improve

www.ingramcontent.com/pod-product-compliance
Lightning Source LLC
LaVergne TN
LVHW051734050326
832903LV00023B/917